Where People Live

by Margie Burton, Cathy French, and Tammy Jones

We live in all kinds of places.
Some people live
by water.

Some people
live on land
that is high.

Some people
live on land
that is flat.

Look at me!

I live by the ocean.

It has a lot of water.

It is very big.

I like to play in the sand
and the water.

Look at me!
I live by a lake. A lake can be little or big. It has land all around. I like to go for rides in the boat.

Look at me!

I live by a river. The river is long. It takes water to lakes and to the ocean. I like to play in the river.

Look at me!
I live on a hill. The hill
goes up high. I like to ride
my bike up and down the hill.

Look at me!
I live by the mountains.
A mountain is very high.
It is very cool here.
In the winter, I like
to play in the snow.

Look at me!
I live on a plain.
The land is very flat.
You can see things that
are very far away.
I like to help
my grandma
on the farm.

Look at me!
I live in the desert.
It is very hot and dry.
We do not get much rain.
I like to ride my horse
all around.

Look at me!
I live in a forest. A forest
has many trees all around.
It rains a lot here. I like
to climb the trees and play
in my treehouse.

Ocean

Lake

River

Hill

Where do you live?

Mountain

Plain

Desert

Forest